RAINBOW STUDIES INTERNATIONAL

A Special Gift

Presented to

From

On the Occasion of

Date

Gifts for the Family™

"Gifts of Hope™" Series

Compiled by Billy & Janice Hughey

Creating Colorful Treasures™

Gifts for the Family ™

from the "Gifts of Hope™" Series
Copyright © 1997 by Rainbow Studies, Inc.
All rights reserved.

Published by: Rainbow Studies International, P.O. Box 759, El Reno, OK 73036

THE RAINBOW STUDY BIBLE®
Copyright © 1981, 1986, 1989, 1992, 1995 and 1996
by Rainbow Studies, Inc. All rights reserved.

Color Coding System, Bold Line® Words of Trinity System,
Book Outlines and Sectional Headings.
Copyright © 1981, 1986, 1989, 1992, 1995 and 1996
by Rainbow Studies, Inc. All rights reserved.

No part of this book may be reproduced in any form without permission
in writing from the publisher, Rainbow Studies International.

Scripture taken from the HOLY BIBLE: NEW INTERNATIONAL VERSION®. NIV®
Copyright © 1973, 1978 and 1984
by International Bible Society.
Used by permission of Zondervan Publishing House.

The "NIV" and "New International Version" trademarks are registered in the United States Patent and
Trademark Office by International Bible Society.

Verses marked (TLB) are taken from The Living Bible © 1971.
Used by permission of Tyndale House Publishers, Inc., Wheaton, IL 60189. All rights reserved.

Design Concept by Rainbow Studies International and Design Life Studio.

ISBN 0-933657-57-9

Library of Congress Catalog Card Number 97-76616

1 2 3 4 5 6 7 8 9 - 01 00 99 98 97
Rainbow Studies International, El Reno, Oklahoma 73036, U.S.A.

Printed in the United States of America

The "FAMILY" Themes

FAMILY ~ GENEALOGIES ~ MARRIAGE

SEXUAL CONCERNS ~ CHILDREN

PARENTHOOD ~ HOME ~ ADULTERY

FORNICATION ~ DIVORCE

FRIENDSHIPS ~ RELATIONSHIPS

Just follow the Yellow "Quote" Road!

PARENTHOOD

*If you want your **children** to keep their feet on the ground, put some **responsibility** on their shoulders.*

Abigail Van Buren

*Children are a gift from God;
they are his reward.
Children born to a young man
are like sharp arrows to defend him.
Happy is the man who has his quiver
full of them . . . .*

Psalms 127:3-5 TJB

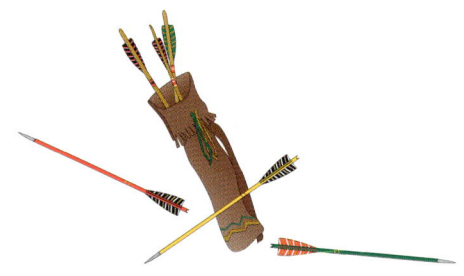

CHILDREN

Life is a **flame**
that is always **burning** *itself out,*
but it catches **fire** *again*
every time a child is born.

George Bernard Shaw

*A baby is God's opinion
that the world should go on.*

Carl Sandburg

*Train up a child
in the way he should go:
and when he is old,
he will not depart from it.*

Proverbs 22:6 KJV

PARENTHOOD

A child can **ask** *a thousand questions that the wisest man cannot* **answer**.

Jacob Abbott

CHILDREN

*Children have more need of **models**
than of critics.*

French Proverb

*Children have never been very good at listening
to their elders, but they have never failed
to **imitate** them.*

James Baldwin

Youth is, after all, just a moment, but it is the moment, the **spark** *that you always carry in your* heart.

Raisa M. Gorbachev

You don't have to

suffer

to be a poet.

Adolescence

is enough suffering

for anyone.

John Ciardi

CHILDREN

Teen-agers *were put on earth to keep adults from wasting time on the* telephone.

Anonymous

CHILDREN

Any child can tell you

that the sole purpose of a middle name

is so he can tell when he's really in trouble.

Dennis Fakes

Cleaning your house while your kids are still growing

is like shoveling the walk before it stops snowing.

Phyllis Diller

*There is only one pretty child in the world,
and every mother has it.*

Chinese Proverb

*Parents of young children should realize
that few people, and maybe no one,
will find their children as enchanting as they do.*

Barbara Walters

Making the decision to **have a child** *— it's momentous. It is to decide forever to have your*

go walking around outside your body.

Elizabeth Stone

PARENTHOOD

When you are a mother,
you are never really alone in your thoughts.
A mother always has to think twice,
once for herself and once for her child.

Sophia Loren

Biology is the least of what
makes someone a *MOTHER*.

Oprah Winfrey

PARENTHOOD

Could I climb to the highest place in Athens, I would lift my voice and proclaim —

 **fellow-citizens,**

why do ye turn and scrape every stone to gather wealth, and take so little care of your children, to whom one day you must relinquish it all?

Socrates

PARENTHOOD

*There are many ways
to measure success;
not the least of which is the way
your child describes you
when talking to a friend.*

Anonymous

When I was a boy of fourteen, my father was so ignorant I could hardly stand to have the old man around. But when I got to be twenty-one, I was astonished at how much he had learned in seven years.

Mark Twain

*I am not **young enough** to know* EVERYTHING.

Oscar Wilde

Fatherhood *is pretending the present you love most is* soap-on-a-rope.

Bill Cosby

*When I was a kid, my parents moved a lot —
but I always found them.*

Rodney Dangerfield

The greatest thing
a father can do
for his children
is to *LOVE*
their mother.

Josh McDowell

PARENTHOOD

Where does the **family** *start?*

It starts with a young man

falling in love with a girl.

No superior alternative has yet been found.

Winston Churchill

Therefore shall a man leave his father and his mother,

and shall cleave unto his wife: and they shall be one flesh.

Genesis 2:24 KJV

FAMILY & MARRIAGE

A successful marriage

requires falling in love

many times,

always with the same person.

Mignon McLaughlin

The **Christian** is supposed to love his neighbor,
and since his wife is his nearest **neighbor**,
she should be his deepest love.

Martin Luther

Making marriage work
is like running a farm.
*You have to start all over again
each morning.*

Anonymous

MARRIAGE

Even if marriages

are made in heaven,

man has to be

responsible *for the* **maintenance**.

James C. Dobson

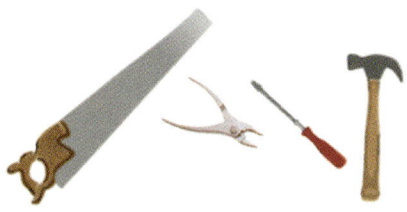

MARRIAGE

*Before marriage, a man will lie awake all night
thinking about something you said;
after marriage, he'll fall asleep
before you finish saying it.*

Helen Rowland

... ZZZ ... Z ... ZZZ ...

*Why does a woman work ten years
to change a man's habits and then complain
that he's not the man she married?*

Barbra Streisand

MARRIAGE

A married couple

that plays cards together is

just a fight that hasn't started yet.

George Burns

MARRIAGE

Marriage is like twirling a baton,
turning handsprings,
or eating with chopsticks;
It looks so EASY *till you* TRY IT*.*

Helen Rowland

*Children often hold a marriage together —
by keeping their parents*
too busy *to quarrel
with each other.*

Anonymous

By all means marry;

*if you get a **good** wife, you'll become happy;*

*if you get a **bad** one, you'll become a philosopher.*

Socrates

More marriages might survive if the partners

realized that sometimes the BETTER

comes after the WORSE.

Doug Larson

MARRIAGE

HOME

*So many persons
who think divorce a panacea
for every ill find out,
when they try it,
that the **remedy** is worse
than the disease.*

Dorothy Dix

*However often marriage is dissolved,
it remains indissoluble. Real* **divorce,**
*the divorce of heart and nerve and fiber,
does not exist, since there is no divorce from memory.*

Virgilia Peterson

"I hate divorce," says the LORD *God of Israel . . . .*

Malachi 2:16 NIV

A house without love

may be a **CASTLE**,

or a palace,

but it is not a home . . . .

John Lubbock

Where is home?

HOME *is where the* HEART

can laugh without shyness.

Home is where the heart's TEARS

can dry at their own pace.

Vernon G. Baker

*A man **travels** the world over in search of what he needs and returns home to find it.*

George Moore

Mid pleasures and palaces though we may roam,
Be it ever so humble, there's no place like home.

John Howard Payne

HOME

Though it rain gold and silver
in a foreign land
and daggers and spears at home,
yet it is better to be
at home.

Malay Proverb

HOME *is the place where,
when you have to go there,
they have to take you in.*

Robert Frost

*It takes a heap o' livin'
in a house t' make it* **home**.

Edgar A. Guest

When home is ruled according to God's Word,
angels *might be asked to stay with us,*
and they would not find themselves
out of their element.

Charles Spurgeon

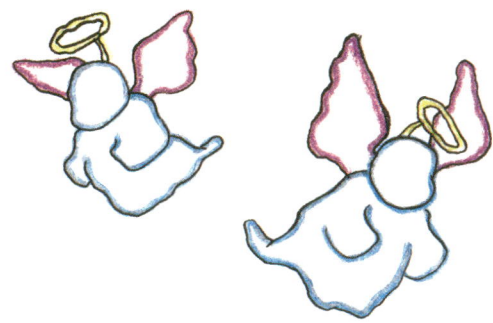

*When you finally go back to your old **hometown**, you find it wasn't the old home you missed but your* childhood.

Sam Ewing

HOME

Nobody can do for little children

what grandparents do.

Grandparents sort of **sprinkle stardust**

over the lives of little children.

Alex Haley

A **grandmother** *is a person with too much wisdom to let that stop her from making a fool of herself over her* **grandchildren**.

Phil Moss

Grandchildren don't make a man feel old; it's the knowledge *that he's married to a grandmother.*

G. Norman Collie

To be **seventy** years young

is sometimes far more cheerful and hopeful

than to be **forty** years old.

Oliver Wendell Holmes, Sr.

Midlife crisis *is that moment*

when you realize your children and your clothes

are about the same age.

Bill Tammeus

FAMILY

There is nothing more **sad** *or* *glorious* *than generations changing* **hands**.

John Cougar Mellencamp

FAMILY

*Parents who wonder
where the younger generation is going
should remember where it came from.*

Sam Ewing

*I don't know who my grandfather was;
I am much more concerned to know
what his grandson will be.*

Abraham Lincoln

GENEALOGIES

You can't expect to make a place

in the sun *for yourself*

if you keep taking refuge under the family tree.

Claude McDonald

GENEALOGIES

Before most people start boasting
about their family tree,
they usually do a good pruning job.

O. A. Battista

Ancestry is most important to those
who have done nothing themselves.

Louis L'Amour

Noble and common blood is of the same color*.*

German Proverb

GENEALOGIES

FRIENDS are FAMILY

you choose for yourself.

Jane Adams

If one falls down, his friend can help him up.

But pity the man who falls

and has no one to help him up!

Ecclesiastes 4:10 NIV

FRIENDSHIPS

A friend hears the

song in my heart

and sings it to me

when my memory fails.

Anonymous

A loyal friend laughs at your jokes when they're not so good,

and sympathizes with your problems when they're not so bad.

Arnold H. Glasow

You don't need to be a friend to everyone.
Remember the model of Jesus.
He preached to, ministered to,
and healed thousands of people,
but he only had **twelve disciples**.

Jim Conway

FRIENDSHIPS

Friends are lost by calling often and calling seldom.

Scottish Proverb

The best mirror is an old friend.

George Herbert

It takes a long time to grow an old friend.

John Leonard

If you want an accounting of your worth,

count your friends.

Merry Browne

friends

are those rare people who ask how we are and then wait to hear the answer.

Ed Cunningham

FRIENDSHIPS

Lots of people want to **ride** *with you in the* **limo**, *but what you want is someone who will take the* **BUS** *with you when the limo breaks down.*

Oprah Winfrey

FRIENDSHIPS

And **ONE** *standing alone*

can be attacked and defeated,

but **TWO** *can stand back-to-back and conquer;*

THREE *is even better,*

for a triple-braided cord is not easily broken.

Ecclesiastes 4:12 TJB

He liked to **LIKE** *people,*

therefore people liked him.

Mark Twain

I have room for one more friend,

and he is **EVERYMAN**.

Woody Guthrie

RELATIONSHIPS & FRIENDSHIPS

*You can make more friends
in two months
by becoming more interested
in other* **people**
*than you can in two years
by trying to get people interested in you.*

Dale Carnegie

FRIENDSHIPS

There are *two types* of people —
those who come into a room and say,
"Well, here I am!"
and those who come in and say,
"Ah, there you are."

Frederick L. Collins

RELATIONSHIPS

Well, enough about me.
Let's talk about you.
What do you think about me?

Bette Midler

We had a lot in common,
I loved him and he loved him.

Shelley Winters

We **agree** *completely on everything, including the fact that we don't see* eye *to* eye

Henry Kissinger and Golda Meir

RELATIONSHIPS

Tact is the art of making guests feel at home when that's really where you wish they were.

George E. Bergman

Do not use a hatchet to remove a fly from your friend's forehead.

Chinese Proverb

*If you think
it's hard to meet
new people,
try picking up the wrong
golf ball.*

Jack Lemmon

RELATIONSHIPS

*If I'm such a legend, then why am I so **lonely**?*

Judy Garland

RELATIONSHIPS

> *'Tis better to be **alone**, than in bad company.*
>
> George Washington

RELATIONSHIPS

Don't urge me to leave you or to turn back from you.
Where you go I will go,
and **where you stay** I will stay.
Your people will be my people and your God my God.
Where you die I will die, and there I will be buried.
May the LORD deal with me, be it ever so severely,
if anything but death separates you and me.

Ruth 1:16-17 NIV

RELATIONSHIPS

*If I had a single flower
for every time I think about you,
I could walk forever
in my* **garden**.

Claudia Grandi

RELATIONSHIPS

Not many sounds in life . . .

exceed in interest

a **knock** *at the door.*

Charles Lamb

RELATIONSHIPS

Why can't we build orphanages next to homes for the aged? If someone's sitting **in a rocker**, *it won't be long before a kid will be* **in his lap**.

Cloris Leachman

*There are no illegitimate children —
only illegitimate parents.*

Leon R. Yankwich

*Flee from sexual immorality.
All other sins a man commits are outside his body,
but he who sins sexually sins against his own body.*

1 Corinthians 6:18 NIV

Samson, for all his **strong** *body,*

had a **weak** *head,*

or he would not have laid it

in a harlot's lap.

Benjamin Franklin

Can a man hold fire against his chest
and not be burned?
Can he walk on hot coals
and not **blister** his feet?
So it is with the man
who commits adultery with another's wife.
He shall not go unpunished for this sin.

Proverbs 6:27-29 TJB

ADULTERY

*How many homes are broken
because of men and women
who are unfaithful!
What sin is committed
every day at this point.
God will not hold you guiltless!*

Billy Graham

ADULTERY

The Bible has a word to describe "safe" sex: It's called marriage.

Gary Smalley and John Trent

SEXUAL CONCERNS

The *husband* should fulfill
his marital duty to his wife,
and likewise the **wife** to her husband.
The wife's body does not belong
to her alone but also to her husband.
In the same way,
the husband's body does not belong
to him alone but also to his wife.

1 Corinthians 7:3-4 NIV

SEXUAL CONCERNS

Give the gift that shows that special someone
how much you care!

Other "Gifts of Hope™" Series Selections

GIFT BOOK — *Gifts of Love*™

GIFT BOOK — *Gifts of Faith*™

GIFT BOOK — *Gifts for Life's Journey*™

Perpetual Calendar

Blank Journal

Available at fine bookstores nationwide
or call 1-800-242-5348

Creating Colorful Treasures™

Give the gift that shows that special someone how much you care!

Additional Rainbow Studies Products

❧ *A Rainbow of Hope*™

❧ *The Rainbow Study Bible*®

- *New International Version* • *King James Version*
- *The Living Bible* • *Reina-Valera Revisión 1960, Spanish*
- *Portuguese*

❧ *CD-ROM – The Rainbow Study Bible® – Parallel Versions by RainbowSoft*™

- *New International Version* • *King James Version*
- *Reina-Valera Revisión 1960, Spanish*

❧ *"In The Beginning" Children's Video Collection*

51 Animated Biblical Stories of the Old & New Testaments. Available in English or Spanish.

Available at fine bookstores nationwide
or call 1-800-242-5348